Unspoken Words

Thea Nikitis

Contents

Dedication

To Alex, my brightest sunshine.

About the Author

Born in 1979, Thea Nikitis travelled and lived in several European countries, including Greece, Germany and Austria. She is a finance specialist at a German bank and lives in Germany with her husband and son.

Chapter 1

It was a bright Sunday morning. Nikoletta looked through the window. There were children on the playground rounded with big beautiful green trees. Nikoletta was looking at kids playing. *There is something magical in children's play,* she would think. It always had a soothing effect on her. Everything seemed so peaceful and calm, yet, today, she was restless.

Nikoletta loved watching children playing on this playground. Her balcony on the third floor of a building overlooked a large playground with many playing possibilities. On this playground, she used to play as a kid. All the children from the neighbourhood would run down to play 'in front of the building'.

The children would sum up in front of the building for uncountable adventures: they were chasing each other, playing hide-and-seek; while were exploring the frogs in the nearby pond, they found a lost dog, fed it, tried to find a home for it and gave him the name Rex. They were coming down with food for Rex every day, knocked on the doors of almost all the neighbours to finally find the family willing to take the deserted Rex.

There were no cell phones at the time. TV was also mostly boring; there was always some grown-ups program, with cartoons playing only from 7 pm to 7.15 pm. After that, it was time for all the children to go to bed.

The divorce of her parents somewhat overshadowed her beautiful childhood memories. Her dad explained that he could not be together with her mum anymore. Her dad was her hero. He often played with her, and he always had some interesting games. They went hiking on the nearby mountain; they visited Children's Theater plays on the weekends; it was always a lot of fun with dad. So, when he said he didn't want to be with Mum anymore, Nikoletta accepted it. She raised no further questions. Little of it she could understand. She did not try to; she was six years old.

The following summer, just before starting school, she went three times on holiday: once with Mum, once with dad and once with the kindergarten. It was awesome. Kids envied her. So, she thought, there are no major downsides to having divorced parents. It was strange, though, on the first day of school, her dad was not there when all the parents came along.

Nikoletta asked Mum, "Mum, will they accept me to school when dad is not here?"

Her mum was heartbroken, but she smiled and answered, "Of course, honey. Nothing can stop you from going to school, don't worry."

Nikoletta was very much looking forward to starting school. Especially since she could read and write already, she started reading early and loved reading; it became her favourite free-time activity in the years to come. It also hugely helped her not to think about her family situation.

At first, she barely noticed that her parents had divorced. Nothing actually changed: she lived in the same building, had the same friends, her dad was always more absent than present at home, so she did not notice his absence. Even before the divorce, he was mostly away from home, doing some important business. When he would come, he would come to their home; nothing much changed.

However, after the divorce, her dad started neglecting her. He would not come up when they agreed he would pick her up; it was with considerable delay even if he came. She waited in front of the building for hours, not allowing her mother to come down and wait with her. Once, she went up to the apartment shortly only to see her father's car driving away from the street. She ran like crazy behind the car. Eventually, her father spotted her and said casually, "Why did you run? I would have driven by again."

The thing was, she could not be sure of that. She could not be sure any more her father would keep his promise.

This was the period when she started reading. Books would bring her into a different world, an exciting world, a world of phantasy, the world she liked and where she felt safe and did not feel neglected. Through books, she learned to also deal with negative feelings and see different perspectives on everything. The world of books was to become her safe world from everything unpleasant that might be happening.

She was not told the exact reason for her parent's divorce. She saw her parents arguing a lot. Her father would always try to offend her mum by saying, "You have big feet, you have a big nose," as if it was important at all.

"If he is bothered with her feet or nose, why did he marry her in the first place?" Nikoletta thought in dismay.

One night, Mum and Dad were arguing a lot. Nikoletta tried to go to bed, but she could not fall asleep from the noise from the living room. She opened the room door slightly to see what was happening and saw Mum and Dad, both on their feet, quarrelling about something she could not see. She put the pillow on her head not to hear the noise and eventually fell asleep.

The reason for the divorce could not stay hidden from her forever. After a while, she found out her father had an affair. And that was not a one-night-stand affair; it lasted for years. For three years, he lived a double life with her mum and the other woman. Her mum figured it out based on a book that was suddenly missing from her shelf in the apartment and miraculously appeared on a colleague's desk from work. Her mum got suspicious and started interrogating. She was sneaking his bag, which he always held with him, away from her, found many phone numbers. One of the numbers was from the colleague who had her book, Zinovia. Figuring out that the disappearance of the book and remarkable discovery of it on Zinovia's desk are a reason for concern, Nikoletta's mum dialled the number. She started the conversation casually:

"Hi, I just wanted to tell you, Giannis and I are over. We will get a divorce soon. Now you can be relaxed and tell me what is going on."

Zinovia, as she was not very smart, bit and explained everything: how they fell in love, how they have been seeing each other for a couple of years now, how they are planning to get married.

"Interesting," Nikoletta's mum answered. "Hasn't it occurred to you that he already has a family?"

On the verge of tears, she exclaimed, "You disgusting bitch!" and broke the line.

However, Zinovia did not last for long. Although it was expected that once Giannis was divorced, he would marry Zinovia that did not happen. They broke up soon afterwards. It turned out that Zinovia had affairs with many married men at the same time, so Giannis broke the relationship with her, simultaneously breaking their family as well.

Afterwards, her dad started having many girlfriends. Nikoletta met almost all of them. They were very young, considerably younger than he was, always smiling, and very nice to her.

He was very generous with them. He bought cars, apartments, paid for weekend trips, and uncountable nights out.

Besides bringing her to his girlfriends, dad had less and less time for Nikoletta alone.

Chapter 2

Nikoletta and Mark met at a friend's birthday party for the first time. Previously he saw her holiday photo, which her best friend Anna was showing along with other photos to friends.

"Great photos, Anna! Who is this beauty here?" Mark asked.

"Oh, no, Mark, it's forbidden. She is young and inexperienced…"

"…and very attractive! Can you introduce us? I would like to get to know her."

"Sure, sure there will be a possibility. Just pay attention, she is young she is not one of the girls to play with."

"I know what I am doing." Mark smiled. "Just introduce us." He smiled again.

Anna and Nikoletta were the best of friends. Their friendship started in kindergarten and was only getting stronger with the years. Like little children, they would gather old things and try to sell them in front of the supermarket nearby to buy presents for their mums for Mother's Day. Or they were sneaking into ruined buildings in the neighbourhood, thinking they would find Frankenstein there and trying to find him. They never talked about the school. Nikoletta was doing well in school, Anna less, but diverging interests in school did not impair their friendship a bit. As they grew older, they went out together all the time. With her beautiful blue eyes, Anna was attracting a lot of attention from the boys, shy Nikoletta less. Her deep dark brown eyes were full of mystery, simultaneously glowing friendliness and warmth. However, her profound beauty was captivating only for those daring to look. Nikoletta was always closed and stayed at a distance; not many were bold enough to approach her.

Their differences did not impair the relationship between Nikoletta and Anna. Every holiday they would spend together, having fun meeting new people, enjoying the beach, and dancing every night.

Mark was a well-known guy in the city. He was the best friend of Ana's brother. That is how he got to see Nikoletta's photo. Early in his youth, he started gaining a lot of attention from the girls. They all seemed to want to be with him. Although not particularly interested in any of them, he liked and enjoyed the attention and was with many of them. For him, it was all just a play until he found the right one sometime in the future. Seeing Nikoletta's photo, he was captured instantaneously. The warmth, the energy, friendliness sparking from these beautiful eyes left him speechless. He wanted to get to know this beautiful girl as soon as possible.

Nikoletta was also full of anticipation to meet him and see what would happen when they met in person.

When she saw him, at first, she was mostly confused. Everybody said he was handsome, although she could not see that at first glance. He was interesting and attractive, but she could not define what made him so interesting. He looked like a nice guy, but why were so many girls interested in him? There were a lot of other nice guys around, she thought. Other girls saw something special apparently: he was among the most desired young men in the city.

And he noticed her. He noticed her; the girl grasped in books and school and, as she thought, generally uninteresting for the boys around. He was six years older, which made him even more interesting. An older guy liked her and asked about her, the guy everybody knew and liked in the city. This made her restless. She did not know what to feel or how to react, not to mention what to do. She was sixteen years old at the time.

The atmosphere at the party was very lively. The birthday boy's friends gathered all in one room, took their shirts off to make their masculine photos, laughing loudly. Girls were sitting in a corner, drinking champagne, and discussing each other's clothes and makeup. Nikoletta did not know which group to join. Therefore, she just took her drink, stayed in the middle of the room, and started dancing a bit. Dancing relaxed her always; she was in a good mood. She did not notice the boys around looking at her with admiration, Mark most of all.

"Hi, I'm Markos," Mark approached her "you can call me Mark." With that smile, Nikoletta was already interested.

"Nikoletta," she responded with a smile.

"How a beautiful name," he noticed.

"My dad gave it to me. My parents agreed if the baby is a boy, my mum is choosing a name for him. If it is a girl, dad is choosing. So, dad got the chance to name me." Nikoletta was smiling.

"Nice," he responded, "another drink maybe?"

"No, thanks, I'm fine. Do you like the party?"

"Hehe, it's cool. A lot of hormones playing in the other room." He smiled.

"Ah, that. Well, the most important is they are having fun," she answered with another smile.

"Mark, come immediately. I need you," his sister Maya called.

At that moment, Mark said to Nikoletta, "Excuse me. See you later around," and went away to help his sister.

By the end of the evening, they did not talk much; they smiled fondly at each other instead.

The next opportunity for them to meet was another birthday party. A friend was celebrating his eighteenth birthday and invited many friends. Nikoletta was looking forward to it; she was looking forward to continuing their conversation, wondering what Mark would say, what he would do, and if he took the next step, hoping secretly he would ask her out or he had too many girls in his head and would not bother with Nikoletta anyway. He was known in the city as a womanizer. What he said about her, he said probably for many other girls. Only for her, it was the first time, and for her, it was special. She was contemplating what to wear and practising what she should say if he asked her out, but her best friend Anna had a fight with the birthday boy's sister Helen over a birthday present.

"Hi, Anna, I know we agreed to buy a present together," Helen said. "Only, I've talked to my parents. They think we should buy a present together as a family."

"But you promised to buy a present with me!" Anna responded, clearly annoyed.

"I know, I know, my folks are adamant, so I have to buy with them. Hope you will have a good time at the party," Helen concluded.

"No chance I am going. This is betrayal. I'm out" Anna was furious.

Not being well acquainted with the birthday boy, Ana felt left out and thought it would be better not to go. Somehow felt stupid. Anna did not want to go anymore.

However, Nikoletta had a different opinion. She did not care about presents; she wanted to see Mark and continue talking to him. She liked him so much!

For Nikoletta, it was fine that Helen bought a present with her parents. Unusual would have been that she showed up with a smaller present with Anna; she saw no reason for being upset.

She was contemplating to go the party alone. After all, she knew all the people. She found it stupid to think about what she would do there by herself, with no one to talk to for longer than a minute or two. She did not feel confident enough for that.

So, in the end, Nikoletta did not come to the party either. Only afterwards did she hear from friends that Mark asked about her.

"How stupid," Nikoletta thought. "Now I will not see him."

"How stupid that I did not go," she contemplated further, "maybe Mark would be with me the whole time."

"But then, maybe he does not want to be with me the whole time, and I end up alone." She was running in circles.

She wanted so badly to meet him, to hear, what he would say, to see what he would do, would he ask her to be his girlfriend… Or she was only dreaming way too much.

However, she needn't wait long to see him again.

One day, going back home from school, she saw him in a car. He saw her too and waived. She was so excited from only seeing him that she didn't take her usual nap that afternoon after school. Sleeping was out of the question. Everything was out of the question. Mark waved to her. She wanted so badly; she wanted it all, a boyfriend. She wanted Mark to be her boyfriend and to take her everywhere. She wanted to go with him everywhere. She could not stand the anticipation. She knew already what made him so interesting among the girls. His deep green eyes, sharp look, his half-smile – and you are knocked down before you know it. Nikoletta was. She was so excited from the sole expectation and wondered what could be. She did not know how she should behave, though. She was sixteen years old.

They met in the city cafes many times afterwards, but Mark did not make the first move. He would greet her politely, exchange a few words and nothing more. Although she liked him a lot, she concluded he was not interested in her.

Chapter 3

After multiple coincidental encounters in the city cafés and restaurants involving many of their mutual friends, a new opportunity came for them to have time to speak to each other in private. It was a hot August Saturday evening, they were out in a café, and Nikoletta had just come back from the summer holiday, where she went with Anna. Mark and his friend saw the girls and approached them, offering a drink, as it was custom. And they started talking, drinking, and dancing. Nikoletta and Mark talked about the summer holidays; he was at Mykonos, she at Chalkidiki. He was thrilled with the parties in Mykonos.

"You can't imagine it. It is nothing like here in Thessaloniki, where the parties are usually great. It's a whole different world; everybody is so relaxed or drunk. I couldn't say," he smiled and continued, "everybody is dancing and singing and doing whatever they want, whereby others barely notice or not notice at all. It's freedom on a completely different level. And parties are literally everywhere. You should go and see. I'm sure you would like it," he said.

"Hmm… I think I would," she smiled. "Anna and I also had an awesome holiday. The best so far. We rented a motorbike and visited the other villages in Sithonia. Once I met and shook hands with guys on the highway, it was so relaxed. Anna was laughing at the bare idea of it on the front seat," she continued, "we were going out every night, God, we met so many people. One night we met a group of guys from Thessaloniki we know; they said - you two are not eating anything; you are living on calories from vodka. That was not very far from the truth." she smiled again.

"Fancy a dance?" he asked.

She smiled. These eyes, this smile. "I would go with him to the moon," she thought.

But they did not make it to the dancing floor. His face was so close she felt his breath. She smelled his perfume. He was so close that a "should I try?" thought crossed her mind at the very moment when he kissed her.

It was the best kiss ever. "The feeling of having him near me, his masculinity, and his strength," Nikoletta was above the seven skies. It was the best kiss ever.

They kissed passionately for the rest of the night. Not noticing people around, not noticing music, not noticing anything.

His hand slid under her shirt in the dark corner of the café, where nobody was looking. Nikoletta felt excitement as she never did and continued kissing him passionately. For the two of them, they were alone in the universe. And it was perfect; it felt like heaven. She wished it would go on like that forever.

Now, at almost seventeen, she knew she was in love. Years later, in hindsight, she understood, at first glance, Mark was not really an eye-catcher for her; somebody would say he was average. But at a second glance, when you look at him, really look at him, you realize there was something magnetic about these deep green eyes and this half-smile; he draws your full attention, and you only want to be near him, to hug him, to kiss him.

"How lucky! I would have taken a second glance; now I'm captured," Nikoletta thought years after that.

Chapter 4

The next day he called her and asked her out. She, of course, happily accepted.

"Wow, now I have a boyfriend," she thought.

He came with a car to pick her up, gave her a small kiss on the lips, and then they headed to a popular café Game. The conversation was easy and simple. Nikoletta wanted to show that she was not too excited and mature; therefore, she kept talking about anything that crossed her mind, which happened to be school topics mostly. She could not help it; her whole world was books and friends, now she started talking about school, unconscious that that might not be the best topic for a date. It was of utmost importance not to show how excited and nervous she was, so she kept talking to avoid the awkward silence.

The school, however, was not the best topic to start with Mark. He struggled with a difficult relationship with his dad, sensing that he was having an affair, and revolted, so he did not devote himself to the university the way his father wanted out of protest. Nevertheless, he said nothing and let Nikoletta happily chat on the way.

They met a mutual acquaintance in the café who said, without much consideration, "Hi, how come you two are together?" Like if it was a miracle that they would be going out.

Nikoletta's hart sank. That was it. They do not belong together. Everybody knows she is not in his league. She was uninteresting, average-looking, nerd crazy about books, and he was the most popular guy in the city, whom every girl wanted. Of course, they did not belong together. What was he doing with her after all?

Mark, however, did not seem to pay much attention and continued talking to her. On the way back, he said goodbye and kissed her on the lips in the car.

After that, he did not call again.

Nikoletta was waiting for the call. She was very disappointed. She was embarrassed. She goes on a date with a guy, and after that, he doesn't call ever again for whatever reason.

"Am I so boring? What have I done wrong? If he doesn't want to see me anymore, wouldn't it be nicer to call and explain?"

She would have understood. She understood already that some girl much cooler and more popular would fit better with him. This was such a disappointment. She went through the entire conversation of that evening many times in her head and could not find any clues. He simply did not like her, she concluded. Probably he was drunk when he kissed her, so it doesn't count. It never counted. Only she wanted it to count. It was all fiction in her head; he was never serious about her.

Finally, she accepted he would not call anyway, especially after the friend's comment. He was never really interested in her; she was too young, too uninteresting, and too focused on school, which was definitely not the favourite topic among young people at that time and at that age. So, she continued her life, going to school, having fun with her friends, trying to forget him, and dreaming of him secretly at night.

She did not take well such a rejection. Knowing that she liked him and wanted to be with him, and he, suddenly, for no reason, does not want her was painful. Not knowing what she had done wrong did not help. She was clueless about what had happened; she sought an explanation she was not receiving and had to move on.

Being surrounded by many friends helped her a lot to forget. She was still thinking about him, but so many happenings in and outside the school helped suppress her disappointment deep down.

Mark, on the other hand, liked Nikoletta as ever. On their date, he realized that she was very young and innocent. His experience with girls was mostly with older girls who knew very well what they were doing and had already had some experience. Nikoletta was a completely different story. He felt, all of a sudden, a concern not to hurt her inadvertently. She was so special that he, although having quite an experience, did not actually know how to behave. Her talking about school made him insecure. Especially since his university record was not actually representative, he was simply not that good at the university and didn't want to be. This was his way to prove that a faithful husband was more worth it than a good student. He struggled with exams; he would pass at the end of the year, but not with flying colors.

Nevertheless, he liked Nikoletta a lot. "What experience brings after all," he thought. "I have been with girls that do not count, really. When you meet someone so special, you are just like a scared teenager," he criticized himself.

They met the following January again when Anna was turning eighteen. All her friends were at the party, at least all who mattered, Mark inclusive. Nikoletta was trying not to show any feelings, not to mention anything about her and Mark's single date that was a failure, and in all those attempts, she perhaps drank a vodka or two too many. She decided not to pay too much attention to Mark, and vodka helped. She was dancing, having fun, tried not to look in Mark's direction.

As she was a bit tipsy, she went out to the balcony for fresh air. Mark followed. She was pleased to see him and have the opportunity to talk to him in private, hoping for an explanation.

"Hey," said Nikoletta.

"What's up?" followed Mark. "A vodka too many?"

"No, I just went out for some fresh air."

"It's a great night," said Mark with his deep voice, "unlikely warm for January."

"Yes," she said. "Having fun?"

"Yes, a nice party, I would say."

"Only Anna's boyfriend, Dimitris, seems to have drunk too much, is my impression."

"Don't know; I wasn't paying attention," she responded.

After a minute's silence, he continued, "Nikoletta, that in autumn..."

"That in autumn, it wasn't supposed to happen: It was a mistake…" she interrupted him.

"It was not a mistake for me; I knew what I was doing very well."

Their conversation was interrupted but the unpleasant noise from the bathroom. It was Dimitris throwing up.

They both smiled awkwardly. "Obviously, you were right about that one," she said.

But Mark continued, "I knew very well what I was doing. I like you. But you were talking about the school…"

"Well, of course, that's my life. I'm going to school every day…"

"Sure, sure," he responded when Anna interrupted, coming out to the balcony. "Nikoletta, you will freeze. You are in a simple shirt and look how cold it is."

Although it was warm for a winter night, it was very cold for simply wearing a shirt. Nikoletta did not feel any of it, but they went in nevertheless. Without anything being explained.

Mark knew very well what he was doing indeed. He liked Nikoletta a lot; no other girl could compare to her. She was younger, and his mother warned him to pay attention, not to do anything if he was not serious about her. But the thing was, for the first time in his life, he genuinely wanted it to be serious. He wanted Nikoletta. After meeting her, he thought only she might be too young for a serious relationship; he decided to wait a bit. He wanted to tell her how much he liked her, how special she was to him. He wanted to explain but somehow could not. He did not know how to explain that he felt somewhat insecure talking about school, so in the end, he did not explain anything at all. Now she was hurt.

Nikoletta was trying to find clues in whole happenings. What does that mean, "I knew very well what I was doing?"

Why hadn't he explained? When he did not kiss her by coincidence, why aren't they together now? And what was so wrong with her talking about the school?

"It was only a chat. You can talk about whatever you want." Nikoletta's thoughts ran around in all directions without a clear goal or conclusion. However, she would have loved to have come to a conclusion.

She never asked him any of it. Nikoletta understood nothing. Somehow, we did not click; after all, she thought again. He is probably not really interested in me; he is only being polite. That was the only conclusion she was coming to in the end.

Days went by. Winter turned into spring. Mark did not call. They occasionally met now and then in the city but without talking to each other.

Nikoletta was progressing well in school. She liked it a lot and tried to do the best she could.

From her early childhood, Nikoletta was attached to books. The books were her backup world; there was no room for pain or sadness that might come up in real life; there was so much room for imagination; there was so much content and peace in books. Being transferred to a different world with happenings unrelated to her own life calmed her. From books, she learned how to deal with unpleasant situations and feelings.

Although not aware of it, books have become her secret escape with time.

Chapter 5

Spring was there; the trees turned green, flowers in thousands of colors were blooming, people were gathering in café gardens that had just been re-opened, and the positive atmosphere was everywhere.

At school, spring means the spring excursions that so many students are looking forward to. Nikoletta's class was going to Athens this year. She was very much looking forward to it; she adored Athens.

Her two school best friends, Maria and Theodora, were not coming. They decided on another excursion to Budapest, but most of their classmates were coming along, "It is going to be perfect," she thought.

"Athens is always a good idea. With so much culture, wisdom of ancient times, great ancient architecture, one could not make a mistake with Athens," Nikoletta thought.

Everybody was in a good mood; the class gathered at a bus station to start their trip to Athens. Many of Nikoletta's friends were there, making arrangements about who would sleep with whom in a room. Nikoletta agreed to be in a room with her class friend Gianna.

At nights, Nikoletta and Gianna would talk a lot, mostly about boys. Nikoletta confessed to Gianna about Mark.

"Nikoletta, who is that perfect guy that you are so successfully hiding from everyone? He must be something special," said Gianna.

"Oh, he is very special to me, Gianna. He, ahm, he has this look in his eyes; you see that he looks at you fondly, and at the same time, you have no idea what he is up to," Nikoletta responded sincerely.

"And he is always so cool… kind of unapproachable; can't really say whether he likes me."

"Well, you like him a lot, obviously," Gianna was teasing her. "Does he know how you feel about him?"

"Hmm, I never said it directly, but he could read the clues if he is interested."

"Let me tell you something, Nikoletta. Men are not that good at reading clues. He needs to see and feel a green light from you to make the first move. They are also insecure," Gianna continued.

"Oh, Gianna, so many girls are always around him. He cannot be insecure," Nikoletta said with a slight sadness in her voice.

"Still, that does not necessarily need to mean a lot. Greenlight, Nikoletta, if you care, let him see the green light from your side – a smile, a comment, come closer to him; he has to feel it," Gianna concluded.

The conversation made Nikoletta realize she was far away from being over him.

On the first day of the excursion, they passed by Meteora, a rock formation with ancient monasteries built high on rocks, and spent the day there. Nikoletta watched the rocks that endured so many centuries, thought about the Monks and the way of life they were leading, and wondered how it was like to live such a life in solitude, away from people and civilization. The peace they experienced, the serenity. She thought it would be nice to occasionally run away from the chaos of life, from everything that worried you, and wondered whether they were running from something in their lives when opting to live such a life…

On the excursion, they all had a great time. They reached Acropolis on the second day. Acropolis was stunning as always. Nikoletta could not explain this magnificent feeling when standing there. Suddenly, she would feel freedom from all constraints and all worries, surrounded by the thoughts of culture and history, imagining what it was like when Socrates and Aristotle walked on these rocks. She felt so empowered.

"How much wisdom was exchanged on these rocks? Why don't we have such wisdom now? Why aren't people walking in the streets now discussing important topics in life such as happiness, democracy, and order of a state? Did they invent everything, so we do not need to think and develop further? What made the people of that time so wise? They were so advanced back then. Based on what, can we repeat it now," she was thinking. However, the crowds were so annoying that she promised herself again to come here and enjoy the beauty in peace sometimes, when not too many visitors were coming, which was almost never, but definitely worth a try.

The excursion was empowering experience for Nikoletta. She had time to think things through and see different perspectives in her life. She thought about Mark a lot. Her thoughts were always how she wanted him by her side. But she realized that it was not the end of the world if it did not happen. She will be fine, nevertheless.

When they came back to Thessaloniki, Nikoletta started, surprisingly to her, to gain increased attention from the boys. Usually, her two best friends were the 'interesting ones,' she reckoned, and she accepted her fate as 'nerd' and 'boring.' She invented that for herself. However, nobody ever said or hinted at anything like that. Now it was different. Many boys approached her and showed her their interest. And she accepted, to go out at least. She finally felt like the others, and although she was not interested in the particular boys approaching her, she agreed to go out on a date just to see how it felt. It tuned out that it didn't feel any special. In her mind, Mark was still making himself comfortable; no one could beat him. Not even come close. Nikoletta herself was unaware of how much in love she was with Mark.

In summer, just before the summer holiday, Nikoletta met Michalis. She liked him, and he liked her as well. They started going out just before Nikoletta went with Anna to Chalkidiki for the summer holiday. He was talking to her about everything. They would go to the Thessaloniki fortress Heptapyrgion and talk about the Ottoman times; they would go to the seaside to eat gyros at a place Michalis claimed had the best gyros in the city. They laughed and had a good time together, and he was a great kisser.

Nikoletta liked Michalis, really liked him, she thought. "Just to get away from thoughts about Mark," she thought as well. Michalis was a great-looking boy, very tall, extremely attractive. "He is better looking than Mark," she thought. "Mark will be jealous when he sees us together," she continued thinking, "He will realize what he has lost."

She promised him to write a Chalkidiki card and call when she was back.

None of it did she do.

Just the night after the girls came back from the summer holiday, while Nikoletta was sitting in a popular café with Michalis, suddenly, out of nowhere, Mark appeared. He hugged her tightly from the back so that she forgot in a moment everything, sang a line in her ear, she inhaled his presence, smelled his skin, she wanted him so much, and all thoughts about Michalis were blown away in a second.

Michalis figured out what was going on and discretely went away from the table. She did not miss him for a second. Mark was the only one in her mind again.

Her whole world was Mark. She tried to deny it, convincing herself that she was not interested in Mark, but her mind and feelings had another tune. She was over and over drawn to him; she couldn't get him out of her mind.

"How does he do it?" Nikoletta thought, annoyed. "Who gives him the right to do that to me? When he does not want me, I am entitled to have another boyfriend. He just appears and brings a mess in my head, a mess in my life, only to disappear again…" She was desperate, she could not help it, when Mark appeared, she forgot about everyone and everything. As if someone threw a spell at her.

Chapter 6

Soon thereafter came her eighteenth birthday. The long hoped for eighteenth. She invited all of her friends, from more cities even. Some of them even came from Athens. Holiday friends, school friends, neighborhood friends, all. And all of them came.

Many asked Anna for a hint regarding birthday presents, so in the end, Nikoletta received all the things she really wanted.

Of course, she invited Mark as well. She craved for him to be there. He was important to her; he had to come. And he did. Seeing him appearing with a bottle of martini, she knew he was the only one she wanted. Difficult that would change, she realized meanwhile.

She called him right before the party to ask whether he could bring some music. "He, folk music, then," he said, "that's all I have."

"That will be a hell of a party then," she responded.

And it was, indeed. After the music started, the friends who were not that delighted with folk music wrote on a paper "we were listening to Vassilis Karras here" and photographed it so that everybody knew afterward.

As the party progressed, everybody in a good mood, empowered by vodka, whiskey, or martini, whatever they were drinking, sang along to “Girise, sou leo Girise…” and had a great time.

Nikoletta wore a hell blue dress that suited her perfectly. It was an excellent combination with white shoes for her special night. Mark came with a bottle of martini and a huge bouquet of violet flowers, handsome as always. “He remembers that violet is my favorite color,” Nikoletta thought excitedly.

Mark’s eye was red, but when the others asked what happened, he responded nonchalantly that he had slept on by the draft. Well, not very likely, many of them thought, but it stopped further questions.

During the evening, Nikoletta went to the kitchen to bring some drinks for the friends, and Mark was already there. “Hey you,” she said, “enjoying the party?”

Actually, she was so happy that he was there. She was looking for him the whole evening.

“You look marvelous,” he responded, “and the party is great, by the way.”

“Hehe the music contributed to the mood considerably,” she smiled.

“Some more beer?” Nikoletta asked, taking a glass from the glass case.

"Nah," he took her in his arms from behind. She turned around; their faces were so close. She inhaled him again. He gave her the most beautiful and the most meaningful kiss.

And they started kissing. Passionately. They were so much into each other that he decided differently when Mark's friend Giorgos came in to take another drink. They were not to be disturbed. They looked perfect together. They were so meant to be.

"They want each other so much; can't they see that," Giorgos thought. Nikoletta and Mark didn't stop kissing till the end of the night.

After that night, they were together again. For Nikoletta, that was the best birthday and best night of all times. Being with Mark made her happy and excited as she had never been before.

Days went by, and they started seeing each other and going out together more frequently. Each time they would go out, they ended up in his apartment kissing and taking more and more clothes off.

They started being relaxed with each other, just wearing underwear. Once Mark was contently walking through the apartment with only the boxer shorts on, she read aloud.

"Mr. Big," she smiled brightly. "Well, hello, Mr. Big," she started teasing him.

"That's how you advertise yourself," she was still smiling.

"Hehe, not really. It's only for a special girl to be seen."

"Wow, special girl. How special?"

"So special that I like her so much, I like her so much that I cannot stop thinking about her, and I always want to grab her…"

He grabbed her with both his arms and kissed her passionately.

"And do some interesting stuff with her" He took her with his arms and carried her to bed.

"What interesting stuff…" she uttered excitedly.

"You know, the grown-ups stuff…"

One night at his place, it almost came to it. But Nikoletta was not ready to go till the end. She had so many questions unanswered. She wanted confirmation that she was the only for him; she was to lose virginity to the one who meant serious to her.

But although it was true, Mark did not read the signs. He said nothing of the things she so desperately needed.

She knew everybody had done it before, and she was madly in love with Mark but was hesitating, seeking confirmation.

She was insecure; would she be his girlfriend now? His one and only girlfriend? Is he capable of it at all? Is he willing? Now she knew; he often said he liked her, but was that enough, shouldn't there be more than simply liking? How many of us does he just "like?"

She did not bring out that topic when they were talking.

After a couple of weeks, her determination weakened, the desire was stronger, and she concluded she would do it anyhow. She realized that she was ready and won't think that much, she loved him, and he should be her first.

And it happened. On a long autumn night, they spent it together. And it was marvelous. Mark was very caring and careful; he was considerate, and she was the first to lose her virginity to him. He was with many girls, but Nikoletta was the first virgin. He knew that it hurt and was extremely careful. They were both partly insecure, but it all turned out good in the end. He was very happy, finally something that meant that he was special to her and that she really liked him. She was happy to have shared it with Mark, the only one who mattered to her. "Now I am not a virgin anymore," she thought contently, "and Mark is my man."

She talked about it with Anna. They were happily making jokes about future mutual holidays with their boyfriends, Mark and Nikos, Anna's boyfriend who came after Dimitris and with whom Anna was very much in love.

A couple of days afterward, he called her, but she got the flu and could not meet him.

"Hello, Mr. Big," she said when answering the phone. He laughed. She remembered him having underwear that had "Mr. Big" written on it, and they both found it funny. Anything was funny for them at the time; they were in love, only Nikoletta did not realize that. She was subconsciously afraid it was impossible he would be in love with her; he always had so many girls.

The thought of him being a womanizer was detrimental to their relationship. She could not get rid of the thought that he had many others, and it was an extremely unpleasant thought. She always thought she was not special enough for him, she was not good enough… and could not relax and simply enjoy their relationship.

After a couple of days spent at home ill, she started thinking. So many questions were in her head again; she was insecure. She had to come clean about what was actually happening. This was quite exhausting without really knowing if they were really together or not. She needed confirmations Mark was unaware of; she was overthinking everything while he thought they were progressing well.

The next time they met, she asked, "What are we now? Are we together?"

Apparently, he was better prepared for that conversation than her or simply had more experience. He responded, "What would you like us to be?"

He didn't want to be completely open in the case she did not share his feelings. And Nikoletta backed, afraid of the unwanted answer, afraid not to embarrass herself.

"I do not want a boyfriend now."

"I cannot have a girlfriend now either. I have so many obligations," he continued the game.

So, the conversation was closed before it began, without anything being really said.

They saw each other a couple of more times after that, and then once Nikoletta said, "I cannot do this anymore. I mean, you have tons of girls, and I am seeing only you. Drive me home."

"I am not seeing tons of girls; I don't understand where you are getting it from. It is not true," he responded, but she was not listening. She was deeply hurt. She did not realize she was hurting herself.

Mark was confused about Nikoletta's behavior. He did not know what to think. He liked her very much but could not understand her. She acted as if she wanted to be with him, then suddenly withdrew. All these talks about him having many other girlfriends were complete nonsense. Yes, he attracted a lot of attention from the opposite sex and had a couple of them, but he was not a womanizer. He wanted to get serious with Nikoletta; she had the warmest eyes and the friendliest smile. He was so attracted to her the chemistry between them was unbearable. At the moment he thought they were going somewhere, she comes, doesn't want anything anymore but to break up.

Why can they not be dating like millions of other people? It was stupid. He sensed that she liked him. He read her desire when her face comes close to his. "Maybe I misread the signs because of my own desire," he thought. He thought they were so meant to be, but somehow it did not work. So, he drove her home that night and went on without her.

He confessed his feelings to Giorgos, his good friend.

"I don't know, Giorgos. This girl drives me crazy," he said once over a beer.

"She is so young, so gentle, so warm… I like her so much."

"Are you sure 'like' is the correct word," Giorgos started teasing him. "Why don't you tell her how you feel?"

"Oh, no, man, that is impossible. If she does not feel the same, she can start mocking me, telling her girlfriends, I don't know…" Mark responded.

"But how do you ever know how she feels? Someone has to take the first step… Taken that she is only eighteen…" Giorgos did not finish the sentence.

"Since I am older, I shall be a cool guy, don't I? And not be running around her as a monkey…" Mark was in thought.

"Hm, yes and no, my friend. Playing it cool might end up totally cooling her off. She might understand you are actually not that interested," Giorgos said.

"I don't understand what is going on in her head. If only I could…"

Mark stayed confused. He realized that many misunderstandings were going on, but at the moment, he did not dare to straighten it up.

In the meantime, Nikoletta tried hard to forget Mark. It was not meant to be, she would repeat to herself. She was going out, amusing herself, he was always somewhere in the back of her mind, but she used her whole willpower to push him away.

Days became months, and months became years. They were away from each other. Their adventure seemed forgotten in the past. Nikoletta had other boyfriends. Mark had other girlfriends.

However, in the end, none of it did work out. Yes, the other ones were good and smart, but Nikoletta could not settle with one of them. She could feel as happy, safe, and fulfilled with no one else as with Mark.

Chapter 7

In these days, Nikoletta's desire to continue her studies abroad matured. Yes, she will do a master's in one of the most developed countries in Europe, for example, the UK or Germany or some other European country. The idea became her obsession. She wrote to all famous universities in Europe, from Ireland to Austria, inquiring about entry requirements and scholarship possibilities. Although a very successful single mother who was earning really a lot, her mum could not finance her studies abroad.

That did not stop Nikoletta. She started inquiring about scholarship opportunities. "There are many scholarships in Europe," she thought. "I only need to get one."

She could not admit that she wanted to run away from her family situation with divorced parents and dad in the arms of many different women. She felt embarrassed about that, with no fault of her own. She sought to make it all good and have a fresh start by herself. In a world she creates for herself, without the burden of the past.

After a couple of years, one late summer night, she and Anna met Mark in a café. They sparkled within a moment, so thirsty for each other, so wanting, so desiring each other. The old story continued almost instantaneously.

They started seeing each other again. This time it was different. They were older; they knew better what they were doing, and… the sex was magnificent. It needed just Mark's touch, and a thousand lights went on throughout her body. Every time they met, she wanted him so badly that she couldn't put her hands off him. Mark experienced the same. Yes, he had lots of girls, but he felt he could conquer the world with Nikoletta in his arms. "It is magic what's happening; this girl is my soul mate," he thought. "If she only wanted it," he continued thinking.

"It was marvelous," he would say to Nikoletta afterward.

"If that were the sole criterion to choose a partner for life," she said once to Theodora, "then Mark and I are meant to be."

This time Mark and Nikoletta saw each other on a more profound level. There were no other girls mentioned. There was no "he likes me; he likes me not," they were simply going out together, drinking coffees together, having a good time together. He always had time for her whenever she called and spent time with her. Other people, when they saw them together, were all, "Oh, you two again, it's always you two," and Nikoletta asked herself whether they knew something she did not. They were referring to them as an item. And she loved the idea of being an item with Mark.

At this time, Nikoletta was finishing her bachelor's and fine-tuning plans for master's studies abroad. She dreamt of foreign cities, different languages, new cultures, and foreign friends; she wanted to broaden her horizons and gain more knowledge. Most of all, she dreamt of creating her own life without the burden of the past. She wanted to run away from her dad. She did not want anyone to connect her with him in any way. Ever. She was intensively looking for a scholarship. Nikoletta was persistent. She wrote to many famous universities to inquire about scholarship possibilities and entrance criteria.

As her idea about studying abroad developed, Nikoletta realized that summer programs at foreign Universities would help her realize her goal.

She enrolled in a German university summer school held in her home city Thessaloniki. The summer program consisted of five days of lectures and workshops. Students from neighboring countries Bulgaria, Macedonia, Albania, and Turkey were also attending. One day, the leading professor said to students, "If you wish to pursue your studies in Germany, just let me know," That was enough for Nikoletta. She approached him after the lecture, saying that she wanted to enroll in a master's studies program in Germany. "Oh, well, let's go have coffee somewhere then," and they went to a café nearby. He inquired about her motivation, her determination, and her studies.

"There are always many applicants, but it's worth trying," he said. "You should pay attention to submitting all the required documents and being in the correct order. Besides, the better you can speak German, the higher your chances of a scholarship."

It was a pleasant conversation. Nikoletta felt the support of the professor. He took her questions seriously and tried to explain things in detail. "On the website of the DAAD, this is the agency for student exchange; you will find all application documents. Pay close attention to doing everything correctly and neatly. That leaves a good impression. You should find a lector of the scholarship provider. There should be one in Thessaloniki. If you are determined, you will succeed. And do not pay attention to what other people are telling you. Follow your goals." Nikoletta wanted to do only that. Follow her goal, whatever other people are thinking.

She remembered every word the professor said correctly, found the responsible person at Thessaloniki University, started taking intensive German classes, and applied. "I want to broaden my horizons. I want to meet new people. I want to make foreign friends. I want to learn finance in the most developed countries in Europe," Nikoletta thought while writing her graduate Thesis about European Monetary policy and taking intensive German classes.

She confessed to Mark about her application for a German scholarship. He was so attentive and listening every word. He even went with her to the university to ask additional questions about the scholarship.

“Sorry Mark, I am really bothering you. That is always on my mind. I want it so badly.”

“No, not at all. I find it interesting,” he would respond, giving her his support.

She nicknamed him Schatz as she was all about Germany these days. He called her Schatz back.

They would lie on the bed and talk about foreign cities and cultures for ages. Nikoletta would always conclude that Greece is the best country in the world. Mark was more drawn to faraway destinations.

He never asked her if she would get this scholarship and go to Germany, whether she intended to come back after her studies or not. It was somehow self-understood that she would be back. He wanted her to come back.

Chapter 8

One day her mum said, "Nikoletta, we need to talk. I have something to tell you."

"Sure, Mum, what's up?" she asked.

"It is rather serious. Try to stay calm. Your father is in prison."

"What? How do you know that? That cannot be true. What could dad do to go to jail?" Nikoletta was furious and on the verge of tears. "How do you know that? How long has he been there? What did he do? This is not happening."

"It is still under investigation. Apparently, he signed some forbidden documents," her mother responded.

"This is hell. When is he coming out? Maybe after the investigation, they will conclude he did nothing wrong and let him go," cried Nikoletta.

"Don't know, sweetie. Let's hope for the best. There needs to be a trial first. The lawyers will be involved. I hope he gets himself a good one. I hope he'll be out soon as well."

After a couple of months, her mum found an article in the newspapers. It stated that Nikoletta's father was sentenced to seven years in prison.

"Nikoletta, can you come, sweetie? I need to show you something," she started.

"Yes, Mum?"

"Maybe you should read this," she said. "I'm so sorry; I don't know what to do."

"How could this happen? I don't understand. What was he doing? What was he thinking?" Nikoletta was extremely upset after having read the article.

After a while came a letter for her from her dad. It said:

"Dear Nikoletta,

I know this is very strange and unexpected for you. It was unexpected for me as well.

I will stay here for a little while and am coming out soon. Do not worry about me. I'm fine.

Never forget that I dearly love you, you are my only child, and I will always be there for you.

Yours,

Dad Giannis"

That's ridiculous, Nikoletta thought. *If he really loved me, as he states, he would have thought how it all influenced me when he was doing it. Come on, he never actually thought about me. He is only capable of thinking of himself and talking about love,* she thought. *Ever since I was six years old, he has always cared only for himself and his needs. Does he even know what love is?* she was extremely angry. *And since when is seven years a little while,* she sadly wondered.

Nikoletta was devastated. If it was in the paper, everyone could read it. Her friends could read it. Mark could read it. Will they still be her friends when they read it? She was deeply upset. Why can't this man let her live her own life freely? He is always burdened with happenings in his own life; she is the one to suffer from it. She is the one to bear the consequences of his misdeeds. That is so unfair. And then he comes and talks about love. How much has she suffered from his irresponsible behavior, his uncontrollable behavior with other women; how much has she suffered already. And now this on the top… crap.

Nikoletta did not know how to behave. What would she say to her friends? How shall she behave now? Like nothing has happened, or come clear and talk about it? She could not talk about it. At the moment, she didn't have a nice word about her father. And talking bad about your own dad only makes things worse.

It was hugely exhausting, so she concluded not to say anything. She did not know what to say anyway. Luckily for her, her friends were polite enough not to mention it.

But she stopped calling Mark. Out of embarrassment. They were talking a lot about everything. She could not say anything, knowing that he knew, and she could not say anything. She was simply ashamed. Mark's had a nice family; his dad was a decent man. "There is nothing wrong with getting divorced when things are not working and finding another person to settle down with," she thought. It is utterly wrong to get divorced, fly from flower to flower, and get involved with many women. And prison in the end. She missed Mark more than anything but did not call him anymore. And he, reading the newspaper and figuring out what was happening, did not call for a while either.

She wanted more than anything to run away. Everything was unbearable. She couldn't stand the situation anymore. She felt so embarrassed. She felt so humiliated as if someone threw a rock weighing 100 kg at her; she felt powerless to move in any direction. She craved to talk to somebody about everything, but embarrassment stopped her from confiding to any of her friends. She increasingly felt lonely with only one huge desire to get away from it.

After a while of feeling utterly insecure, she gathered her strength and started calling Mark again. She needed him, she wanted him, she wanted none of this to happen; she only wanted her boyfriend. Dad's imprisonment was official, it was known, and nobody said anything, so she could go on pretending as if nothing had happened. She realized she needed to see the love of her life no matter what her dad did and where he was. That was his life. She decided to continue living her life.

Mark embraced her when she called again. He figured out what was happening and gave her all his support without any one of them ever mentioning her dad. He realized she wanted it that way. If she ever wanted to talk, he would be there for her. This time Nikoletta was seeking more closeness and support. She could stay in bed for a long time just hugging and stroking Mark; he would kiss her all over again. He felt her need for him to be close, and he was as close as ever. He would do anything for this tender, vulnerable creature that heaven sent him. Schatz, she would say, is the German word for honey. Just being with him filled her with positivity; the world would become a safe place when she was in his arms.

She switched her focus from her father to studying abroad and talked about applying for scholarships extensively. It became her obsession and, in her mind, the only way to get rid of all the bad things in her life.

Mark was very supportive. Although he was not in the scholarship subjects at all, he went with her to find a DAAD lector at the Thessaloniki University and talked with her about scholarships for hours. This meant a lot to her because support was more than welcome at this moment. She did not mention her dad. He did not either; she did not know whether he read the newspapers. They were spending a lot of time together. And sex was amazing, as always.

Oh, sex with Mark. She couldn't get enough of it. Exciting, adventurous, and at the same time so gentle and caring. He had the way to light all the lights within her. He had a way to make her forget everything and feel like the happiest on the planet. Every touch was a sensation. Every kiss caused a firework within her body.

They would have long conversations afterward.

She did not get that much support for her studies in Germany from other people. Some friends said at first, "There will be nothing of it. You're dreaming." Even Anna doubted and said, "You in Germany, as if," so Mark was the only one with patience for her constant talk about studies in Germany.

After applying for a scholarship in Germany, she found out she went into the second round and was invited for an interview at DAAD Headquarters in Athens. She went happily.

During the interview, an unexpected happened. She frowned. Her German was well advanced; the interviewers acknowledged that, but the questions about her written graduate thesis from a university she could not answer that well. In a moment, she blocked and forgot some things.

After the interview, the interviewer said, "Do not be afraid next time," and she interpreted that as a bad sign.

On the way back home, she was devastated. She spent most of the time on the bus crying uncontrollably, and then when she calmed down, she said to her mum, who was the other person giving her unconditional support, "I will not stop here. I will apply for other scholarships. This is not the only scholarship. I will find the way."

Although secretly wishing her to stay, Penelope realized her motivations and reasons and gave her all of her support.

For the time being, after the interview. She decided to wait. Somehow could not give up the idea that everything was lost and continued learning German intensively.

As a couple of months went by, Mary, her German teacher, said, "It's over. You received it. Otherwise, you would have received a rejection letter already," Nikoletta said nothing.

Indeed, after six months, when she was coming home from her Aerobic class, her mum called her on the cell phone. "A letter came for you. I do not understand anything, it is in German, but I think you received the scholarship. Come home quickly to have a look." Her instant reaction was to call Mark to tell him, which she did. But she could not reach him. He was not answering.

Overwhelmed with excitement, she did not pay much attention to it. "Wow, this is real. I am really going. Am I ready for it? Oh, yes, more than ready, so looking forward to it," she thought on the way home.

When she came home, her Mum waited for her with a smile on her face. "Here are the sums written. I thought they would not be sending you how much you didn't receive but have a look." Nikoletta investigated the paper and looked and looked. Yes, it was definitely an acceptance. She was admitted to the University of Hamburg; she applied for and got a study scholarship. "Shall I bring some champagne?" mum asked, but Nikoletta was only confused.

So it was real. Nobody believed, but she believed with her whole heart. And it was happening.

Chapter 9

The following months were all about the preparation, visa regulation, and finding a room to live in Hamburg. She was getting ready to leave. The first time alone, in a foreign city, in a foreign country. This thought inspired her.

"Now, at twenty-four, I have the opportunity to form my world the way I want," she thought, "and see what from the old world I will keep and what not. This is my new adventure."

She was looking forward to meeting new people from different countries, speaking foreign languages, and learning new things. There was a lot that motivated her. Nevertheless, she felt awkwardly lonely that Mark was not there to share it with her. It was as if when the prospect of leaving was becoming real; he withdrew; she was wondering whether that was on purpose or not.

Nikoletta felt the need to run away more intensively. The whole fuss about her dad, prison, divorce, she hated it all. She wanted only to be away from this awful feeling of shame. Not realizing what she had done to cause it, the burden of it all was heavy on her chest. She only wanted to be free of all of it, not to feel it anymore. A fresh new start in a new country would help her forget about it all and live freely. A slight shadow of her departure was that she was leaving Mark as well, without explanation. She was trying to rescue herself, and that gained the highest priority. On the other hand, Mark was only slightly aware of any of the things happening in her head.

At the airport, her mum broke. She was so happy and proud of Nikoletta the whole time, but she could not stop her tears at the airport. Nikoletta was surprised. She was so concentrated on getting a scholarship and acceptance from the university that she missed seeing how difficult that was for the mum. “It’s all fine. It’s all fine,” mum said. But the tears would not stop. Only then Nikoletta realized her mum actually did not want her to leave. But she did not deprive Nikoletta of her unconditional support. She did not want to stop her from pursuing her dreams. For the hundredth time, Nikoletta concluded how great her mother’s personality was.

Her mum, Penelope, was hoping Nikoletta would give up the idea of going abroad along the way. Seeing her determination, she did not want to stop Nikoletta in her ambitions; seeing what she was going through and understanding what she probably felt, she had no choice but to be there for her and give Nikoletta her unconditional support. Knowing all of it did not hurt any less. Nikoletta was her precious little girl who was about to explore the whole wide world now. By herself. Penelope loved her dearly and was determined to support her with all her strength along the way.

In the new city, Nikoletta met many new friends. The students' dormitory was full of young people from all over the world, and she found it awesome that everybody was getting along so well despite differences – different languages, different cultures, different confessions… it seemed to make no difference. People were getting along and having lots of fun together. One morning she even saw a couple coming together out of the shower and thought having a boyfriend in a students' dormitory was really cute. However, at the same time, she thought that she would never do it. *"Not my thing"* crossed her mind.

The university was great. She made many friends quickly. She liked the people, and she liked the university. She liked the fact that they were all speaking German with so many mistakes that no one cared about, they were speaking nevertheless, and Nikoletta found it great.

None of the boys she met really appealed to her. Mark fought his way to her thoughts again. Daydreaming how they will eventually somehow be together again after all. Although this was far from probable: he would have put more effort into keeping her if he really liked her.

It was awkward that she left for Germany without a proper goodbye. She called him once. The holiday season came; she went on a summer holiday, and he probably did as well, and they did not get a chance to talk to each other.

In Germany, she continued fantasizing about him.

The move to Germany was way easier than she thought. Just after landing at the Hamburg airport, a couple of fellow students from the student dormitory were waiting for her. Previously she exchanged a couple of emails with them to inform them about the day and time of her arrival. They were very welcoming and friendly, they showed her to her room, and Nikoletta felt good, with none of the awkwardness she expected.

The master's studies started well. She got some good grades at the outset and was putting much effort in. Nikoletta wanted to learn things; she was motivated and found it all very interesting. The effort was not left unpaid. She was also proud of herself that she could have as much success as in Greece, although she was studying in two foreign languages. She found it astonishing that she was talking in different languages with such ease in such a short period of time. She was learning so much that she missed many student parties, although she loved partying. Studying was her priority.

In no time, Christmas time was approaching already. Nikoletta was so excited about going home she could not wait to get on the plane, hear the Greek language again and see her mother and friends. After arriving, she went to a café to meet her best friends. She was just entering the café when Theodora, her friend, pointed out that she should greet someone. She turned around and there he was, Mark. Delighted to see him, she gave him the largest hug, whispering "Schatz" in his ear, the nickname she used when they were together. In a second, he was as close as ever.

She was shining with joy to see him.

"Great to see you," she was shining with joy.

"Great to see you too, German girl. Or shall I say 'wie geht's?' Looking good," and here came his secret half-smile.

"Thanks, well I sleep a lot, every night at 22.30 I'm in bed," she said, smiling.

"We shall catch up while you are here. What do you say?" he asked.

"Great idea, we should do that." She was already looking forward to it.

However, in the end, there was not enough time for it. Nikoletta came for only a week with so many friends and relatives to visit.

One night she invited him to a club where she was meeting a couple of friends. Although accepting initially, he messaged her after a while:

"Hi Schatz, sorry, something came up. I cannot come," he said.

Trying to hide her disappointment, she answered lightly, "Okay, no prob then, next time."

Nikoletta did not expect him really to come. It was kind of unlikely he would. Nikoletta was with other friends there he did not even know. But she was somewhat disappointed, nevertheless. It crossed her mind that he would have come if he cared about her after such a long time. It didn't cross her mind that she left without a goodbye, and he continued the same old game.

Therefore, she returned to Germany and continued her adventure without saying goodbye again. Spring was coming, Nikoletta was having a great time, awesome friends, and at the university, everything was great; she had a lot of success. Every once in a while, she would remember Mark, still wanting that they end up together eventually, still longing for his kisses, still dreaming of his hugs that make her feel so secure. They must end up together eventually. Somehow.

She went on a short trip with university friends to visit Copenhagen in spring. The weather was wonderful. The girls were enjoying the ferry ride when she heard her phone. It was a message from Mark.

"Hey babe, how are you doing? We have beautiful weather here; the girls are wearing short skirts," funny message, she thought. And did not stop for a moment to think whether this message had a deeper meaning. Maybe he was trying to tell her something with this message or to hear from her that she was upset with the fact that he was looking at other girls, to get a message that she still cared, but Nikoletta did not give it much of a thought.

She just responded, “Oh, hi, I’m on my way back from Copenhagen, it is great. Many greetings,” and so it was over, with nothing being said again.

Mark missed Nikoletta. A lot. He was torturing himself with the thoughts of how she met other guys in Germany, how she was probably going out with somebody, how she forgot about him and went into a better world. He sent her a message just to test her reaction. Whether she will get upset to hear he is also looking at other girls, she is not the only one to find new love. He was looking at nobody but craved to get a message from her that she cared. The message did not come. Torn between the desire to embrace Nikoletta in his arms and the wish to continue his life, nevertheless, he found another girl. In addition, he had to stop other people teasing him that he was waiting for Nikoletta while she was kissing other guys far away.

Chapter 10

They met again when she came for the summer holidays to Thessaloniki. She didn't dare call him, though. *We are not that close anymore. It would be strange if I called him now. We shifted away from each other somehow. Especially after that message where he told me he was looking at other girls. That is how much I meant to him,* she thought with dismay.

They met once in the city center street. Nikoletta was with a friend and spontaneously decided to go for a coffee. The next night they met in a club, and lots of other friends were there as well. So, they did not have a moment of their own. But on the way back home from the club, he took her hand. In the club, he was distant, much more distant than previously. Usually, he would have hugged her, kissed her, and shown much more interest in her, but it was different this time. He was just standing there. Now, outside, he said, holding her hand, "My sister says I should marry you," but he did not say either what he thought about it. Nikoletta let it go again, not asking what he thinks. Although actually, that was exactly what he was waiting for, to get a hint about whether she would be interested? Nikoletta still thought about university all the time and was not bothered much with marriage at all. With anyone. Not that she wouldn't be over the moon had he said he wanted to marry her. Most probably, she would have instantaneously forgotten about the university and all. But that did not happen. She just let it go.

Mark was actually testing the field the whole time. He still could not understand Nikoletta. Whenever he tried to give her a hint, wishing to get a sign of her, it ended up as a disaster. She would run away. He brought up the topic of marriage since he was thirty-one, and everybody was talking about it, expecting him to get married. In his head, there was only Nikoletta. Yes, he had this other girl, but he didn't mean it seriously. He imagined his future only with Nikoletta. Only with her he could imagine being happy. But with her so far away and increasing chances that she will stay abroad also after finishing university, his idea of marrying her started to fade away. He didn't want to give it up. That's why he brought up the topic. He wanted her to know that she had the support of his family; it went without saying that he would want that. But she seemed only to be interested in university and her career.

He drove her back home, and they kissed eventually. But it was not as before. Not even similar. Usually, his hands would be all around her. This time not. At first, she thought, *"We are older, we are more mature, and this is how it looks like now."*

Mark was somewhat perplexed about the kiss.

What does it mean anyway? She is going back to Germany. She lives there; I live here," he was thinking.

Kind of feels like she only wants to have some fun during the holiday in order to go back and continue her usual life. What would I have given to be part of that usual life. Therefore he said nothing, feeling that he was losing her.

The next day she found out about the girlfriend. Anna called her and asked, "Did you know Mark has a girlfriend?" That hurt. That really hurt. She felt as if she was cut with a knife.

"Don't worry. It is nothing serious you can blow her away in a minute." But Nikoletta did not listen. It was like an arrow through the heart. It hurt so much.

How can he betray me like this? Why didn't he say, "Hey Schatz, I have a girlfriend?" It was disrespectful most of all. She did not expect him not to have anyone, and she could accept any honest information, but to kiss her and not to say, kiss her so weakly, without passion, and leave her not knowing that he has a serious relationship. She made it a serious relationship instantly in her head. Nikoletta was devastated. She sensed it was serious, and she did not need anyone to tell her that. It was in his touch; it was in his kiss. He needn't say anything…

And she smoked. And she cried. And she decided to forget him once and for all. And not to see him ever again. So deeply hurt she had never felt in life.

Mark did have a girlfriend. But without much meaning initially. He didn't bring it up, as he thought it was irrelevant. If Nikoletta had shown more interest, he would have ended it immediately. However, she showed only interest in having fun with him and going back to Germany. That hurt. One girl he was serious about did not want him seriously. He figured, whatever he did or said, it wouldn't make any difference in the end. So, he didn't say anything.

On the way back to Germany, her phone beeped at the airport. It was Mark apologizing for not coming to meet her and Anna in the city. But it was all over for her. She wrote a short message where she mostly wrote "goodbye," at least in her head. It was over for her, she thought.

And it did not occur to her to ask him what he had to say about the whole thing. Nor has she confronted him about why he behaved in such a manner. She just decided to forget him and never to have anything to do with him again.

She was young; she would forget him; life is full of possibilities, she thought.

Mark had a family crisis at the time and couldn't join Nikoletta and Anna in the café. It was revealed that his father had an affair. Though being as fair as possible in the situation, he said he would leave but settle all of them financially so they bear as few consequences as possible. But his mother was devastated. Although she surely sensed something was going on, she thought it would be a temporary affair; she thought it would not lead to such a huge change in all their lives. Such a huge change in her life. She was crying and screaming uncontrollably. Mark could not leave her in such a state. So, he missed meeting Nikoletta prior to her departure; he needed to take care of his mother.

Unaware of any of it, Nikoletta went back to Germany, thinking she was doing a good job and having to forget him. Forever. The fact that it hurt so much helped her stop thinking about him and start looking at other boys.

In the time to come, Nikoletta was doing everything not to meet Mark. Every time she came to Thessaloniki, she did everything she could to avoid meeting him, coincidentally or not. Wherever she was invited, and there was a chance she could meet him, she didn't come. She did not want to see him. Ever again. The pain was overwhelming. And humiliation. And disrespect. All those things she never expected from Mark. She had to find a way to get over him and go on with her life. There was nothing for her anymore. Only disappointment.

She decided to find another boyfriend. She decided to be happy without Mark.

Chapter 11

And the other boy came not long thereafter, Grylos. He was cute and seemed totally fascinated by her. The way he looked at her and how he spoke to her was a cure to her wounded heart. They met on a school bus. He asked, “Are you going to the Hamburg Uni as well?” and so started the conversation.

“I’m Jack, the real name is Grylos, but I don’t like it. You can call me Jack,” he said.

“You are Greek? Me too! How come you don’t like the name Grylos, it’s a beautiful name!”

“Nah, boring…”

“How dare you say a Greek name is boring? You are Greek. We are a proud nation!” she was smiling.

“Okay, I see we have a patriot here. Yeah, that’s nice,” he smiled as well.

They found out they had many things in common: Jack’s parents were from Greece, and he could speak a little Greek as well. Although funny. Nikoletta found it nice talking to him in Greek. He made her laugh.

Soon thereafter, they started dating. It was nothing like with Mark. She felt so confident, almost dominating, and she liked it. Jack was proud to go everywhere with her and present her as his girlfriend. Dating Jack was easy. He was so attentive to all her needs. He was a good listener and a great conversation partner. During the time of her thesis writing, he had all the patience and was reading her chapters, giving suggestions where he could. And apart from that, Nikoletta felt his support in whatever she was doing. She started believing in her relationship with Jack and thought that is what a relationship should look like. She wanted it to be the right one, away from ups and downs with Mark, away from insecurity, away from constant mixed feelings.

She noticed they have somewhat differing priorities. While she enjoyed studying and working, she needed her friends, music, talking to people, and interacting. Jack seemed to be interested in the job mostly. He wanted to be an investment banker and work in the stock exchange. He liked doing the other things as well, but way less.

“Stock exchange, huh?” she would say. “Are you aware of the working hours there?”

“Yeah, doesn’t matter. I like it so much and am so motivated; I cannot imagine that any other job would make me happier,” he answered.

“And rich,” she continued laughing.

She ignored their differences. She thought it didn’t mean anything that they were different. They are soul mates, and they understand each other. That is the most important.

Nikoletta graduated from university with flying colors. Jack graduated as well. And the question came - where are they going to search for jobs and live? And together, or separate? Separating was somehow out of the question; Jack was refusing it directly, and Nikoletta was way too insecure and did not have the reason to object. She thought, if it happens that they cannot agree to live in the same county, then it be, when they can, then it is okay. While Nikoletta craved to go back to Greece, Jack was very much prone to staying in Germany. She missed her friends. She missed the Greek atmosphere that was nowhere in the world to be found except in Greece, the little things – frequent coffee drinking in cafes in Thessaloniki, going out, and the music… Oh, the music! It tore her heart to listen to Hatzgiannis singing and be so very far away from all of that. She dreamed of the numerous live music evenings, the flair Greece has, and the happiness that she felt nowhere else as pure as in Greece.

She very much enjoyed studying in Germany and having so many international friends, but she knew her heart was where home was at the end of the day. And home was Greece. Home was Thessaloniki. That is where her arguments with Jack first started.

They went for long walks, the same question in the air "where to now?" She argued why life in Greece would be way better for them. He argued why life in Germany would be way better. During all those walks and arguments, it never came upon them that they should probably go separate ways; it was not mentioned as a possibility. However, it was in the air the whole time.

During her master's thesis, Nikoletta conducted many interviews with companies as she was writing a survey about many international companies. She apparently left quite an impression in a couple of them since she ended up with job offerings. And one job was particularly attractive: she got a job in the USA while interviewing for a US company. That was interesting enough for her to temporarily put her cravings for Greece aside: she wanted to go to the United States. Jack was excited as well and started looking for a job in the United States as well.

Chapter 12

Nikoletta was thrilled about moving to the United States. The job was in New York, the city of her dreams. She was already looking forward to long walks in Central Park, visiting the Moma museum, walking in Times Square… all the thing she knew from TV only shall be a reality now.

Jack has got himself a job in New York as well. Nikoletta thought that was a sign they should stay together, ignoring their differences and numerous misunderstandings once again. Other guys crossed her mind occasionally, but she has shaken these thoughts away. She was with Jack, and she was fine. One day, while on a plane to visit Jack's parents, the thought of Mark hit her strongly. All of a sudden, it seemed to her that Mark should have been in Jack's place. She was thinking of Mark's family, how they liked her, how they all welcomed her and hoped she and Mark would stay together, and how good it felt to be with those people… But she shook that thought away as well, convincing herself she was happy and everything was fine.

And she was fine. Jack's parents were nice as well; she felt pleased with them.

The start in the United States was easier than previously thought. Having international experience, Nikoletta had no problems adjusting to the new environment. American environment was especially easy to adjust to. From the moment you step on American soil, you feel welcome. You feel almost at home. All people she met were positive and very nice. “This culture I could get used to,” she thought.

With Jack, it was even better; one could almost not say that he moved; he behaved and probably felt the same as in Germany. And she went on, only occasionally shortly thinking of Mark, the thought she always tried so hard to shake away and never succeeded completely.

The next summer holiday was special for both her and Jack.

They went to Mexico, an undiscovered destination for Nikoletta’s so far. She had a vague impression of what to expect, as many of her work colleagues were spending their holidays there. They chose a holiday in Cancún. Numerous sandy beaches reminded her of Crete, but Mexico had an equally captivating and completely different flair. The beaches were huge. No matter how many people were there, it never felt overcrowded; there was space for everybody.

Jack and she decided to visit some of the ancient Mayan ruins; she always adored history.

They rented a car and visited the magnificent Chichén Itzá. Nikoletta was overwhelmed. Just like she did as a teenage girl on Acropolis, she started thinking about the people who built it this time.

"Fascinating what people did such a long time ago," she started.

"You would think they were underdeveloped, but look at this! I mean, wow! They seemed to be ahead of us," she was thinking loudly.

"Okay, okay, don't exaggerate. I mean, it is really great…"

"Spectacular!" she exclaimed again and decided to keep her thoughts to herself.

One afternoon they enjoyed the sun rays on the beach, and Nikoletta said, "We are Greek. Let's dance, this music is great! Everybody is dancing here anyway."

She was thrilled. Jack found the idea funny, and they started dancing, him following her… and Jack wasn't completely following; he seemed absent somehow… so they both fell in the sand laughing happily.

"Nikoletta," Jack said when he came to breathe, "with you, it cannot be boring. You always have something interesting on your mind. You are, you are…" he paused, thinking. "Let's go to dinner at a Mexican restaurant. You know, with music, good food…"

"Okay, good idea, why not. Tonight?" Nikoletta responded.

"Yes, tonight would be good." Jack was packing his stuff and preparing to go back to the room.

They decided to go to a traditional Mexican restaurant with live music that evening. They went for Hacienda Sisal. Nikoletta was looking forward as she heard that there was live music in the restaurant.

From the very moment she entered the restaurant, she felt special. It was so pleasant, decorated with differing colors, it radiated Mexican spirit from each corner, and she instantly loved it. They found their seats and started analyzing the menu over a drink.

Jack was somewhat confused. She thought he was also overwhelmed with everything.

"Nikoletta," he started. "I… I wanted to tell you, ahm, ask you something."

"Sure what?" she asked lightheartedly.

"Ahm, would you, I mean, do you want to marry me?" he was on his knees.

Now Nikoletta was overwhelmed. Not that the idea didn't cross her mind, but now, all of a sudden, completely unexpectedly…

She said yes. Oh yes, she wanted to marry him. And they kissed. Nikoletta was very happy. It was all coming to its place. She loved Jack, and obviously, he loved her; they were going to get married.

The rest of the holiday was quiet and happy. Nikoletta and Jack chose an engagement ring and started talking about the wedding.

There came the old topic once again – Nikoletta wanted a wedding in Greece by all means, and without many people, Jack was in Germany with his parents and relatives. The wedding preparations turned quickly from planning a happy occasion to a series of misunderstandings.

In the end, they organized the wedding ceremony in Germany and an after-party in Greece to be happy.

The wedding ceremony in Germany was held according to Jack's terms; Nikoletta did not want to engage much. More precisely, the ceremony was held according to his parents' terms. Nikoletta thought it was utterly unfair and was very upset. She was arguing a lot, mostly with herself. She felt it unfair that other people were mixing in her marriage, where that was her most important day, not theirs. Jack was only balancing between both sides.

A thought came to her mind to call the wedding off. She thought that everything was somehow wrong and artificial at the moment. However, in the end, Nikoletta did not do that.

She stuck to her dream of perfection… They will have a party in Greece, which will make up for everything.

The wedding day was bright and sunny. Nikoletta was anxious. Is this really it? For the rest of my life?

But she decided not to give it too much thought. She and Jack were together, they loved each other, and everything else will sort itself out. Somehow.

The celebration was joyous, everybody was happy, and Nikoletta was too. Although the feeling that something was not quite right was always present, she pressed it to the back of her mind and tried to enjoy the celebration. She was getting married to the man she loved. Hey, what more can one wish for?

The subsequent celebration in Greece was also very nice, although Nikoletta, she could not admit it to herself, was not quite happy. But those were surely only the wedding blues. Her friends were so happy to see her married and to celebrate with her. Everything was surely okay.

Chapter 13

Their married life in the USA went on.

They led a quiet life. Largely determined by her job, which Nikoletta didn't mind, she loved her work. She missed meeting her friends more often, but she pressed that thought as well to the back of her mind.

After a while, Nikoletta got pregnant. She was over the moon. She felt almost instantly that she was pregnant, way before any tests. And she also knew that it was a girl, way before the doctor said it was most probably a girl after three months.

She enjoyed her pregnancy, reading books and resting a lot. Her relationship with Jack seemed to be getting better and better; she couldn't remember they had a single row at this time.

And when she came, the small girl with deep blue eyes, Nikoletta felt the happiest and most fulfilled in her life. Her name is Arianna. "My Arianna," she said, "wow, I am a mother now. Let's make me a good mother. I'll do my best to be a good mother," for this precious little baby, for this precious little girl, who was soon thereafter to become her whole world.

However, despite being totally devoted to the child, she and Jack started growing apart. In the beginning, it was barely noticeable, but the distance between them started growing with time.

She started noticing how absent Jack was with a child in the house. He seemed to be working all the time. He would greet baby Arianna when he came from work and soon thereafter go to his room to work. Nikoletta had a feeling he was working all the time. She wanted him to be more present in the family, to spend more time with the child, his playing time with Arianna was pretty much limited.

Nikoletta did not have an understanding of such working hours. Others are also working, others are also doing their best, but people need some free time as well. Everybody is relaxing also. Jack was on the job the whole time. He would play a series on his laptop only late in the evening, absent as well.

In the beginning, Nikoletta was very much upset about his lack of presence. She needed him to be there. She wanted them to be a happy family. As a result, she was sad. Didn't know what was happening. Yes, she was paying way less attention to Jack than before, but they had a child now who needed all her attention. That couldn't be the reason for such a change. And yes, she couldn't sleep with him anymore. After the birth, this lack of wish was normal, but the wish did not reoccur as time went by. She was simply more and more disappointed in him. With time, she realized that the bond she thought they had disappeared. He was evermore a stranger to her. A stranger with whom she has a child.

Jack was only occasionally present with them. Apparently, he had so much work to do. With time, things got worse.

On the one side, parenthood and the presence of Arianna meant the world to her and made her extremely happy and fulfilled. On the other side, the growing distance between her and Jack frustrated her. She was hiding her emotions and often cried at night. The questions from the back of her mind started coming as if they were there somewhere asleep and now got the possibility to come to light.

Is this right? Is he really the one? Has he ever been the one? Or did I make it all up in my mind, longing for perfection that was not around me? Somehow in the back of my mind, I always knew it was wrong, didn't I? And was I deceiving myself into a created picture of happiness that was never real?

In the nights, she was torn. During the day, everything was okay, and she led a normal busy mum's life. Being Arianna's mum made it all way easier. She was devoted to the child. They did so many things together; they went to the playground nearby, met her kindergarten friends in parks, invited friends home, and always had something to do. With time she suffered less, she thought, probably that is normal.

That is life. I just haven't figured it out yet. You marry, you get a child, you raise a child, those are important things, and there is no place for you anymore. Raising your child is you. As if all married couples understand each other perfectly. As if that is important at all, she consoled herself.

Arianna was a great happy child. She had thousands of ways to make Nikoletta happy and used them. She was running, jumping around, and had so many smart comments for her age. Nikoletta was overwhelmed and genuinely grateful for such a child. She wasn't thinking anything more; she was happy and proud to be Arianna's mum.

For years she accepted her role as such, gave Arianna all the positive energy she had, was happy and grateful for such a child and suppressed any other thoughts.

Her relationship with Jack was getting worse and worse. They slept in separate rooms for a long time, without any perspective or wish that they come together. He was becoming ruder and more impatient when talking to her. Whatever she said, the annoying comment from his side: "Do not mix where it is not of your business, I am working, don't disturb me," and, "I do not need your comments." Nikoletta saw it; he was hostile, and it was unbearable.

In these situations, she would withdraw, not wanting to create a row in front of the child.

She actually did not know what to do. The most logical step was to leave him. Nikoletta did not have the strength for the step. Being a child of divorced parents, knowing what she experienced and how her father behaved, she couldn't come round to it. She thought about divorce a lot; however, she did not call a lawyer. The dream of a happy family and a happy life could not leave her.

She was thinking about her and Jack a lot. *We were surely both very much in love when we got married;* she would think, *when did this break? How come we didn't notice all the differences between us? Jack is a good man; he is surely also not happy with the whole situation. How come we came to this situation, and now nobody is doing anything about it? We are simply so different with differing priorities. Why did we not see that before?* Nikoletta was contemplating without conclusion.

On the other side, Jack was very unhappy as well. Seeing Nikoletta paying less and less attention to him, seeing him ever less important to her… Sure it is normal that a child takes most of a mother's attention, especially when so small. He was not a fool and did not have unrealistic expectations. However, something he saw in Nikoletta bothered him. Something clicked in her; he didn't know what was happening. He couldn't see the slightest of interest in him coming from her side. He couldn't process the situation and found comfort in his work. Consequently, he was working more and more.

Contemplating the situation, suddenly, from the most hidden corner of her mind, Mark re-emerged. Only in her thought, but he was more and more present. She tried to stop the thoughts. Mark doesn't exist for you, she repeated to herself.

He is surely happily married and has a great life; how dare you think of him? He is not a single boy you may daydream of; he is a happily married man! Nikoletta would criticize herself. It is a sin. You must stop thinking of him, she ordered herself, but with little success. The thought of him would always come back.

And it was so strong, so vivid. She played so many mutual moments in her mind and how he made her feel. How happy she was when he touched her when he hugged her, when he kissed her. How the kiss felt on her lips…

She tried to stop the thoughts. After a while, she gave it up. It was harmless anyway; she was thinking of Mark in the evenings, she started dreaming of him in her sleep, but it did not affect anyone at all.

In her mind, only after so many years did the events and reasoning behind her come to get another perspective. *After we slept for the first time, when I asked him what we were, he responded, "What you would like us to be?" Maybe, just maybe, he was insecure as well in my reaction and did not want to exclaim, "I want you to be my girlfriend!" Honestly, nobody would have done that. At least nobody with a trace of dignity in himself.*

"And when he kissed me, knowing that he has another girlfriend, he might not intend to be dishonest. Maybe he did not say it because he wanted me to become his girlfriend, and I was in Germany, and it was all so complicated."

In the end, she figured that she should stop driving herself crazy and concluded: whatever it was, most probably I am inventing stuff now when my life did not turn out as expected, but anyway, it is over. Forever over. Nothing will change now. I am married with a child. Mark is surely married with children as well. It shall stay like that.

So she continued like that. For years to come, nothing much changed. Her relationship with Jack did not show signs of improvement. Nikoletta did not want improvement. Jack was ever more distant to her. They were living under the same roof, still sleeping in different rooms, barely talking to each other during the day. When Arianna was present, they communicated more and avoided conflicts. Even if she wanted to talk to him, he would usually say, "I'm working now," indicating that she should not be there. And Nikoletta got used to that. She realized by now that she had made a huge mistake when marrying him, although all with the best and most honest intentions. She shouldn't have married him. He was not the one. And she disregarded it. Mark was and has always been simply the one. She gave it up too quickly, without questions, without clarifications. Probably it would fail anyway, but you do not give up that easily on somebody who meant the world to you, she realized with dismay. Now she has to bear the consequences of her mistakes; now, nothing more can be done.

Jack and Nikoletta learned how to function almost perfectly. They did not argue. They did not fight. There were no lengthy discussions. She was doing her job; he was doing his. Both were very much devoted to Arianna.

It was life without substance. They were not doing things together. They were laughing together only occasionally with Arianna. Jack did not seem to be bothered by that; he was always by the computer engrossed in his work. Nikoletta stopped bothering with the years. It came to her mind that she is leading an empty life, but she hasn't done anything to change it. She was most of all afraid, torturing herself with the question, "How would divorce affect the child? It is written everywhere that children suffer the most from a divorce. Would she turn insecure?" she didn't want to destroy anything for Arianna. She was a great child, she didn't choose the family to be born in, and she should not bear the consequences of our poor choices. So the years went by.

Years went by, and Arianna was already graduating from high school. She, like Nikoletta, was a very good student. At that moment, she was contemplating which university she wished to apply to.

This was a huge step for Arianna, and Nikoletta wanted to support her as much as she could make the right decision. Being a good student at school, Arianna liked almost all the subjects. She was very much interested in most of them, which enabled her to score high grades without too much effort. However, that was an obstacle as well: she could not decide on one topic she wished to pursue her whole life. Nevertheless, Arianna was outstandingly good at writing.

Nikoletta thought journalism or literature would be the best direction for her. Jack had another opinion: IT or similar would be great – she would always have a well-paid job with it. Nikoletta did not want to push anything too much. In the end, it was Arianna's decision. And she was grown up and mature enough for that.

In the end, Arianna decided on business informatics and felt well with that decision.

She was admitted to Berkeley University and was over the moon to go to study in California.

Chapter 14

As Arianna was happily packing her stuff to go to the university, Nikoletta found herself reminiscing how small she was, how cute she was, all the adventures they experienced together, all the play dates, and now, it seemed all of a sudden, she is a big girl moving out. She was, of course, very happy for Arianna. Only a small shiver of sadness overwhelmed her. She will miss her baby girl…

During the days to come, Nikoletta found herself asking: what now? Arianna is leaving home and goes to live in another city to create a life of her own. Nikoletta was very proud of what a smart, independent girl she had become. She and Jack might not have that much in common, but one thing they mastered exceptionally: they raised a good child, a good person. And she respected Jack for that. And loved in a way.

When Arianna left, after a lot of kissing and hugging, Nikoletta told her they would talk every week, and mum would always be there when she needed her. Nikoletta and Jack returned to an empty house. This time the house was more quiet than usual.

Jack went to his room to work. Nikoletta sat in the kitchen thinking, *Okay, I have my job. Finally, I have time for my work.* Nikoletta loved her work. As much as one can love the work, she usually put a lot of energy into it. Now the question was forming in front of her, is the job sufficient?

How do I wish to spend my free time? She already knew the answer.

The following months went by; Nikoletta went to work, read books, and met friends occasionally. Arianna called every week. She was thrilled with the campus, her new friends, her roommates, and what they learned at the university.

Nikoletta was happy, but something was missing. Increasingly she felt an emptiness in her life, and increasingly she felt the desire for Greece. She was craving that sight of endless blue and the clear blue sky becoming one with the sea on the horizon. Slowly the idea of going back to Greece was crawling into her mind. And for the first time, nothing was stopping her.

She talked to Jack. "I want to return to Greece," she said, "this with the US was a great adventure and a wonderful experience, but I'm not getting any younger. I simply want to enjoy my life. You know as well that I cannot do it anywhere in the world except in Greece," Jack was silent.

"What will happen to us if you go?" he asked.

"Is there an 'us' at all?" she responded. He was silent. "I mean it, Jack. This has never been a proper family. We were nothing like a family. We rarely had meals together, not to mention laughing together. We sleep in different beds since who knows when, and nobody objects. This is not it, Jack, and you know it as well," he was silent again.

"Is this the end of us, whatever it is?"

"Well, I don't know, I suppose so. We do not have almost anything in common. We are not spending time together. We just live under the same roof. With child absent, it doesn't make sense anymore."

"Maybe go for a while. Maybe you wouldn't like it as much as you think."

"Maybe. But yes, Jack, this should be the end of us. We wish for different things. We are different personalities. Through the years, we haven't come closer to each other as expected; our differences only widened. I don't think my desire to live anywhere abroad will reappear. I've seen it all. Now I just want to go home, finally," she said. "I'll go now. We process the whole for a while and talk it over when I'm back."

"Okay," he said, and Nikoletta was ready to plan her trip to Greece.

"Hi honey, do you have some time for me? I want to tell you something."

"Sure, Mum, what's up?"

"I'm travelling to Greece for a couple of weeks. You know how I always miss it."

"Sure, Mum, have a great time. And in summer we go together, okay? I like Greece as well," Arianna said, laughing.

"It's a deal. I might end up living there as well sometime," Nikoletta said.

"Oh, that would be awesome, then I would be coming each summer." Arianna was thrilled.

"Whatever you need, just call. Mum will instantly come. Greece is far away, but I am in the US by plane within a day," Nikoletta said seriously.

"Sure, Mum, but I don't think I will need much. Maybe I will have a boyfriend soon," Arianna confessed.

"Oooh, that's something I need to hear about. Pay close attention to what you are doing. Not all people are honest. You know what I have been telling you. Take care," said Nikoletta.

"Sure, Mum, I know: do not drink much, do not let others pay for your drinks, do not go to bed with someone not worth it. You washed my brain with stuff already," laughed Arianna.

"Good so," replied Nikoletta, and she was packing her stuff for Greece.

The flight was longer than expected. Because of the cancellation, Nikoletta waited longer. People were fighting over seats and complaining over food. Nikoletta noticed none of it. She enjoyed being surrounded by the Greek language and felt serenity long forgotten.

They landed in Athens on a bright sunny day. Nikoletta headed to her apartment and briefly called her mum, delighted that she came and invited her for lunch.

After a lot of hugging and kissing and a chat about Arianna and her studies, during a coffee, her mum asked, "Nikoletta, why did you come now actually? I mean, Arianna is away. You have work to do; I don't really understand what brings you here," and then, "don't get me wrong, I am really happy that you came, but you have a husband in the US, I would have expected that you come together at least, if not together with Arianna should she wish to join you."

There it was. The first criticism. She is not allowed to have her own will and needs anymore, Nikoletta thought. Well, that is going to change.

"Mum, I came for myself because I wanted to. I am considering returning to Greece for good," she said. "I simply think I would be happier here. I have experience abroad, lived in many countries, and it was wonderful. Now I just want to be home. Arianna will visit when she can, and I will visit her frequently," she added.

"And what about Jack? I reckon he is not thrilled with your idea," her mum said.

“No, you’re right. He is not. We will see what happens,” she responded.

“Don’t be ridiculous. There is nothing to be seen. I see it already. If you move here, it would mean the end of you two.” Her mother was angry.

“Mum, maybe the end came a long time ago. Let’s not overtalk it,” she concluded.

“Okay, do what you think is the best. But don’t tell me I haven’t warned you. I know you can consider all the consequences of your deeds. Probably there is more on your mind than you are telling me,” said her mum.

“Thank you, mum. Without your support, I would be nowhere. I love you.” Nikoletta hugged her.

The days in Greece were as expected: bright, the sun was shining, Nikoletta was happy simply to be here, to explore Thessaloniki once again after such a long time… Meeting friends was marvellous, they were loud and always had a joke, meeting so frequently compared to the USA, once a day on average. The genuine Greek atmosphere in the evenings, dinners in restaurants with delicious food that usually ended with going to a live music show filled her heart with joy. While working remotely for her current job in the USA, she started exploring work possibilities in Thessaloniki. She was pleasantly surprised that there were many with experience in the USA.

One of those nights at a live music show, she felt hit by thunder. She was sitting with her old friend Anna and listening to the music, ordering her gin and tonic, when he came in. She recognized him in a second. Inexplicable warmth filled her. She was so glad to see him eventually, to see Mark. He noticed her quickly. And watched her. She felt the pleasantness so long not felt. There was so much she wanted to tell him but somehow couldn't. She returned his gaze only, slightly feeling that her legs could not walk properly, not because of gin, but out of excitement.

They went to each other. He hugged her strongly. She whispered only "Schatz," the nickname they used such a long time ago.

"How are you doing, Schatz?" he asked.

"Long time no see," she smiled.

"Let's have a drink together," he invited.

"Wow, we haven't seen each other for such a long time. Where have you been? In Germany, if I remember correctly?"

"Hehe, you remember correctly," she responded, "the whole life happened," she smiled awkwardly.

"Oh, has it already been the whole life?" he was teasing her.

"Yeah, the whole life, Mark. Now, in hindsight, the feeling is that it all went so quickly. How have you been doing?"

"Here and there, always in Thessaloniki. Traveled, but only on vacation. But that is also not that much; I feel when you have Greece, you do not need to go abroad that much," he smiled, "you will, of course, have a different opinion," with that Mark characteristic look in the eyes.

She forgot how much she missed it. She was forcing herself to forget. And now it was there. As stunning as always.

"Hey, let's take an afternoon off and go somewhere nice for dinner. We have to catch up for decades we haven't seen each other. I'll find a restaurant with a view…" Mark said.

"Did I understand this correctly? Are you inviting me to a date?" Nikoletta could not hide the smile on the corner of her lips.

"Oh, God no," he was playing serious, "only a catch up of old friends," he gave her a meaningful look.

"Well, in that case, I accept," she said, not knowing how to interpret it.

"Give me your number, and I will call you tomorrow. We could drive to Chalkidiki, sit on the beach and talk."

"Okay," she said.

It felt like a date, but it couldn't be a date. Mark was pretty much relaxed about everything, so she concluded she would be as well.

We still talked like we were young and single somehow, *it* is *probably not quite okay, but nothing can happen; therefore, let's enjoy the afternoon,* she thought. "Anyway, we will just sit somewhere and talk. Nothing can happen. It will be nice," she thought. However, other thoughts crossed her mind.

"The other night, he was almost flirting with me," she thought, "kind of felt like before, although we are much older and supposedly wiser now," she realized with a tickle of joy. "Nevertheless, we should be careful. He is surely married now. It doesn't stop him from flirting as always. Same old Mark," she thought with a smile on her face. She was simply so thrilled to have seen him. She couldn't admit it to herself.

"Never-ending story of Mark and Nikoletta," she thought, "stop it. It is over. It has been over a long time ago. It is forgotten. He chose the other one over you. Finally, get used to it. It is time for you to forget it."

She didn't dare tell anybody about the agreement to meet Mark. When her head cooled off after the first encounter, she started thinking more prudently. She knew how ridiculous it was. "Okay, there mustn't be anything happening. He might be drawn to me because of the past, but you need to keep a cold head. He is surely married, and if this is the case, it is dishonest just to be going to meet him, not to mention anything else. I am not such a person."

She knew deep inside a part of her never really stopped loving him. Unfortunately, she realized it was too late to do or try anything. The only thing she could do was continue suppressing it, hoping that it would fade away.

"Yes, I love him, but it was always only from my side. This feeling was never mutual. He was attracted to me at best. WAS. Do not forget it," a criticizing thought reappeared. She was preparing for the meeting with Mark at the same time, contemplating that it was a mistake and partly regretting that she said yes.

The next day he called and said he would pick her up after breakfast.

Nikoletta was excited. She didn't know what to expect; as a matter of fact, she didn't expect anything. She was only excited that she was going to Chalkidiki with Mark. She put aside the thoughts of whether it was wrong. She was simply happy to spend the afternoon with Mark. Mark. Her Mark. She wore a light blue dress with espadrilles; she didn't want to overdo it. She did not want to leave an impression that it was more than it was—an afternoon of talking to the old friend, whom she dearly loved and still loves.

When she entered the car, Mark was in a good mood. "Hey, babe, looking good," he said.

"Hi Mark, what's up?"

They drove away for Chalkidiki. Chalkidiki was an hour's drive, just enough for a friendly chat.

"Where are we heading to?" she asked.

"I thought Neos Marmaras unless you have a better idea on your mind," he said, "just around the corner, there is this beautiful beach, and there is a fine fish restaurant on the beach," he said.

"Yes, great idea, remember that place," she responded.

"Oh, it is so good to see you, Nikoletta. I cannot believe that we lost contact for such a long time. I missed you," Mark continued.

Nikoletta was overwhelmed. "Good to see you too, Mark," she responded. With a vague smile.

"And how have you been? Where have you been the whole time? It is difficult to put decades in a couple of sentences but try your best, please," he smiled, driving.

"Oh, yes, good. During my studies I was in Germany, you know that. Afterwards moved to the United States, and I have been working there the whole time. Got a child, a daughter, Arianna. Now, she is really great. She is my sunshine. Now she headed off for University to California," Nikoletta said, "how have you been doing all these years?

What happened in Thessaloniki while I was gone? Always had minimal time to visit, and then it was usually parents, family, and the closest friends…"

"Yeah, I understand that. I can imagine how it is. Suppose you liked it, right? Well, the US, great, that is new for me did not know that you ended on the other side of the pond," he smiled broadly.

"How have I been doing? Hmmm, let's see…" Mark was all smiles.

"Good, I would say. I worked for Mercedes here in Thessaloniki and travelled around. Also got married. A boy and a girl, they are awesome. You should meet them," Mark responded.

"That would be the whole life in a couple of sentences. We made it," Nikoletta remarked, and they both smiled at each other fondly.

"Is the old chemistry creeping in, or am I imagining it? God, I shouldn't overthink that much. I should relax and enjoy…" Nikoletta was captured in her thoughts again.

Whether we will have anything more to talk about for the whole afternoon, Nikoletta asked herself. Although during years she thought she would have so much to tell him, and led numerous conversations in her head, now all of it disappeared. She didn't know what to say. She couldn't bring up the topic of them as a couple. That was somehow long forgotten. They had a great time as old close friends, and she was grateful for it. She felt somewhat perplexed, like when she was sixteen.

When they took place on the beach near the sea, she was startled. The blue sea, the clear sky, that is Greece. She thought once again how great the idea was for her to come.

“How long are you staying this time? A long vacation or a short one? Your daughter at uni, some time for yourself?” Mark asked.

“Yeah, I have some time now. Will see how it goes. I will decide on the way when I’m going back. I can work from here as well. Internet is a great discovery,” she didn’t want to say that she was planning to move to Greece yet.

“I would like to tell you a couple of things,” Mark said suddenly, “it will probably go backward, but I was waiting for the opportunity to tell you this, wanted to tell you so much, now I will not miss a chance to tell you, who knows how soon you will be on the other end of the world,” Mark was teasing her, “it is quite serious, though. Please do not laugh,” he said.

“Of course, I will not laugh, whatever it is,” she confirmed, smiling.

“You know, back then, when we were dating and going out so much and doing everything, you know, well, I was pretty much in love with you. No, wrong, I was head over heels in love with you," he said seriously. "I could not read what you thought or wanted. That drove me crazy. I was playing a cool guy, inaccessible, but in the end, I don't know whether that attracted you or had the opposite effect. After years, I concluded that many things between us remained unsaid and unresolved, and before I could understand what was happening, you were back in Germany. Soon after that, I found out from Anna you have a new boyfriend. It was over for good," he said.

"Mark, Mark," she did not know whether to smile or cry as her eyes were becoming wet, "it was such a long time ago. I missed you a lot, mein Schatz."

"Don't know what happened and why it happened. But now it is well in the past; we cannot do anything anymore but spend a great time together as close friends," she was smiling while fighting tears.

"Oh, Mark," she hugged him.

He hugged her firmly back. And then he kissed her.

It was so overwhelming, forbidden, and yet perfect; she couldn't resist it; the feeling was wonderful. She was again so attracted to him as ever. As if all of it was sleeping somewhere deep inside her and just waiting to be rediscovered. For once, she stopped thinking. For once, she was simply with Mark, the man of her life. Here and now. They were kissing so passionately that someone shouted, hey, you two love birds, take a room. Mark looked at her. "Shall we?" he said with his half-smile on his lips.

"What, take a room?" she uttered between kisses.

"Probably…"

"Not that bad idea…"

And they ran back to the beach hotel behind them.

They were kissing all the way to the room and stormed into it, unable to take their hands off each other. His hands were all around her, holding her tight. His kisses were gentle and full of… love crossed her mind. She didn't dare to think. And the sex was great. They were lying on the bed, still stroking and kissing each other.

"It was always you, Nikoletta. You are the one. One and only for me," he said gently.

She still felt dizzy from all that had happened so unexpectedly, so desired, so wonderful and probably so wrong at the same time.

"I don't want to go back in the past…" she uttered after a while.

"I have been thinking about all so much, had so many things I wanted to tell you, but you were far, far away. I thought I would never get to talk to you again. And here we are, as always, we cannot properly sit and talk without ending up in bed," she smiled.

"Not that bad," he smiled back.

"The thing is, this is actually all completely wrong. We cannot do that. We lost our chance," she said firmly.

"No, it isn't, and we haven't. Unless you want it that way," Mark answered, determined.

"Let's go downstairs to have a proper dinner and talk," he said.

"I know I made a major mistake. And another one is not putting enough effort into correcting it. The thing is, I always wanted only you. And you were always slipping through my fingers to get away… I regretted not telling you that I was kind of involved with another girl when you came back to Thessaloniki. I realized with dismay that that was the final game-changer. Never seen you since and was not brave enough to call you and talk it through. Afterwards, there was no chance. I apologize; I was stupid, insecure, too proud or whatever and then I lost you," Mark started.

"No, Mark, please don't tell me that now. I am thinking the whole time the same thing. Why didn't I tell you that I wanted to be with you after we slept together for the first time? What game was I playing? Why didn't I ask you whether you wanted to marry me when you told me your sister would like us to get married? Why didn't I attack you when I found out that you kissed me while having another girlfriend? I acted according to my assumptions back then, which were highly emotional," she said, "only after a long while I started thinking maybe you didn't mean it that way, and we didn't talk. It would have been much less painful to hear from you that you do not want me or prefer another girl over me, that to suffer the torture of own thoughts in years after that."

"I did not ever prefer another girl over you, Nikoletta. I wanted you. Only you were so inaccessible and in Germany, and I doubted that you meant serious with me. I would have left that girl in a second had you told me that you wanted me," said Mark.

"No, no, no, don't tell me that now," Nikoletta's eyes filled with tears again. Although she promised herself she would not be crying. She ran away from this feeling; she tried so hard to forget him that she was so hurt. Now he is saying that he loved her all the way. It cannot be the truth. That cannot be the truth. She cannot fall for it. She is smarter than that. She couldn't have been that inaccessible; her feelings for him couldn't have been that hidden; in the end, she lost her virginity to him. That means something, doesn't it? Even if she could not believe it, as he says, and she was distant, unreadable and inaccessible, he is the man he should have taken the first step, isn't he? This is not the truth.

"No, let's stop this conversation. Can we please go home now?" she said. He wanted to continue the conversation, but she was genuinely inaccessible this time. They drove back to Thessaloniki silently.

Nikoletta was hurt once again. She suffered again. "This man brings only pain. No one in the world can make me feel like he does. In one moment, he brings me to the moon, and I feel such eternal happiness. In the next moment, he throws me away to the floor so I can only feel failure. And it is always like this. I shall not meet him again. The decision not to meet him again I made so many decades ago was right. From him in the end, I only get hurt," she thought during the days thereafter. She tried not to think of him and met friends to forget as she always did.

Mark, on the other hand, was perplexed once again. Regardless of whether as a girl or a woman, this woman keeps confusing me. I really cannot read her through. She is so beautiful. She is so smart. For moments, I see no confidence in her. She is full of confidence in other moments, especially when she decides to run away. Does she want me at all, or not? Is it possible at all to keep her?

That is when he made a decision. No more reading between the lines. No more hidden meanings. I will tell her honestly everything. She can then do with it what she wants. "I am exhausted of these games," he thought.

He called Nikoletta the next day.

“Hey, hi. I was just wondering whether you have time to meet me again. Today?” he asked. “I need just a little bit will not last long.”

“Haven’t we already said everything that was to be said?” she responded, surprised that he called.

“Not at all, in my opinion. I need only to see you once more. I find it important,” he continued. “So at four p.m.?”

“Okay,” she answered, not sure how to understand it.

“As if I understand anything,” Nikoletta thought. She didn’t bother to wear something special and ended up with a beautiful violet dress that highlighted her deep brown eyes. She was hurt, and she didn’t have the strength or desire to be involved once again in this never-ending network of desire and disappointment, wrong assumptions, and wrong interpretation. It seemed everything was wrong with Mark. Only her desire and her love for him were real. Her love, she thought, you are alone there.

“Looking gorgeous,” said Mark as she entered the car. They drove to a café by the sea just beside the White Tower on Nikis Avenue. It was a lovely peaceful afternoon, but in either of them, nothing was peaceful.

“Nikoletta, I wanted to spend some more time with you. You are a great company,” he smiled flirtatiously.

“So here we are, after all. Want to dance with me?”

She looked at him questioningly.

"Want to dance with me forever? Want to laugh with me, cry, wake up with me, like always?" he was still smiling.

"What we have is real. It has always been real. I want to keep it," he said.

Nikoletta was looking in disbelief. "Mark, it makes no sense now. I love you and probably always have. You lived in my thoughts and dreams for a long time. I was craving so much for you. But now it all doesn't make any sense, yes my marriage is over, but you are happily…" Mark stopped her, hugging her tightly.

"Divorced," he ended her sentence and gave her the most passionate kiss.

"Oh… didn't know that… why didn't you…" he stopped her with another kiss.

"I thought I lost you forever," he said, hugging her tightly. Now no words were needed anymore. Every gesture was worth a thousand words. He didn't want to and could not hide the magnitude of emotions that overwhelmed him. Nikoletta needed no confirmation anymore. "I thought I lost you forever." They were watching the blue horizon.

Nikoletta felt a shiver throughout her whole body. Such a pleasant feeling she hadn't had for ages. And all of a sudden, it all came back to her: she felt like sixteen again, kissing the one she had a crush on. She finally felt at home.

www.ingramcontent.com/pod-product-compliance
Ingram Content Group UK Ltd.
Pitfield, Milton Keynes, MK11 3LW, UK
UKHW020139250726
13967UKWH00002B/761

9 781915 424716